Michigan Fish Species

Game Fish & Panfish

Billy Grinslott & Kinsey Marie Books

ISBN - 9781965098806

Long ear sunfish are small, thin-bodied fish with a unique long ear flap on their gill cover, that how they got their name long ear. They are often mistaken for a pumpkinseed. They have an olive to rusty-brown back, a bright orange belly. They typically reach a length of 4.5 inches. They are mostly active during the day and inactive at night.

The Green Sunfish is blue green in color. It has yellow flecks on both its scales and some parts of its sides. The Green Sunfish also has broken blue stripes which is why some people confuse it with the Bluegill. Green Sunfish are very adaptable, they can live in any body of water that has vegetation or weeds. Green sunfish are opportunistic feeders, consuming insects, small fish, and other invertebrates.

Orange spotted sunfish are mostly found in floodplains of the United States of the Great Lakes. Its beautiful shiny silvery-blue body has reddish-orange spots, which give it its name, orange spotted sunfish. They are usually found in southern Michigan but are too small to be popular with anglers. Their average length is 3 inches. They are a small fish.

The Warmouth is a member of the Rock Bass, Green Sunfish and Bluegill family. They can survive in low oxygen environments while other fish cannot. Warmouth can thrive in muddy water, when other fish can't. Warmouth are often confused with rock bass. The difference between the two is in the anal fin: warmouth have three spines on the anal fin ray and rock bass have six spines.

The bluegill also considered a sunfish is the most popular fish to fish for. They are called pan fish because they are about the size of a frying pan. Bluegills love to eat insects and bugs. They have good vision and rely on their keen eyesight to feed. Three types in this group are the Bluegill, Sunfish, and Pumpkinseed.

The Pumpkinseed is also known as pond perch, sun perch, and punky's sunfish. It can be found in numerous lakes, ponds, and rivers. It is their body shape resembling the seed of a pumpkin, that inspired their name. Pumpkinseed sunfish have speckles on their orangish colored sides and back, with a yellow to orange belly and chest. They are active during the day and rest at night near the bottom or in shelter areas.

White perch grow seven to ten inches in length and rarely weigh more than one pound. They have a silvery body with faint lines on the sides. The white perch is an opportunistic feeder. Young feed primarily on zooplankton and adults feed on aquatic insect larvae, minnows and fish eggs. White Perch is a euryhaline species, inhabiting fresh, brackish and coastal waters.

The two most famous perches are the common perch and the yellow perch. The yellow perch has a brilliant greenish yellow color with orange fins. The yellow perch is the biggest one and can grow to a size of 18 inches. It's also known as the jumbo perch. The other type of perch is the white perch. The largest white perch ever caught in Michigan was a 2-pound, 5.92-ounce fish, measuring 16.25 inches,

The Rock Bass is not actually a bass but a member of the sunfish family. The biggest Rock Bass ever caught on record weighs about three pounds and was a little over one foot long. Rock bass like waters with rocky vegetated areas, that's how they got their name.

There are two main types of crappies. The white crappie and the black crappie. They are also members of the sunfish family. The difference between the white and black crappie is one has dark spots and the other has dark lines and is lighter in color. The white crappie has six dorsal fin spines, whereas the black crappie has eight dorsal fin spines. The white crappie can grow bigger and more of the bigger white crappie are caught in North America.

The sucker fish has the same mouth as a carp. They got their name because their mouth is like a suction cup. They normally are bottom feeders and suck their food from the bottom of the lake. Many people use sucker fish to fish for northern pike and other big game fish. The largest sucker fish caught in Michigan was a Red Horse Sucker weighing 12.3 pounds and measuring 28.5 inches.

The black bullhead and yellow bullhead are part of the catfish family. They usually only grow to about 10 inches long. They use their whiskers to help find food. The bullhead is the most common member of the catfish family. Bullheads live in the water containing low oxygen levels. They can survive on low oxygen areas, where other fish can't.

Flathead Catfish, their body is wide but flattened and very low in height. Both eyes are on the top of the flattened head, giving excellent vision to see upward. Flathead catfish live mainly in large bodies of water like big rivers and reservoirs. They prefer deep pools. The largest flathead catfish caught in Michigan weighed 53.35 pounds and was 48 inches long.

There are several species of catfish. The Channel Catfish are the most fished catfish species with around 8 million anglers fishing for them per year. Blue catfish are known for their size, reaching over 100 pounds. Blue catfish, like other catfish, lack scales and have smooth skin. They have barbels (whiskers) around their mouths, which are used for sensing and tasting food. They are generally slate blue on the back and silvery/white on the underside. The largest flathead catfish caught in Michigan weighed in at 53.35 pounds and measured 48 inches.

Bowfins can breathe both air and water, putting them at an advantage in low-oxygen waters. Bowfins are often described as prehistoric relics. This is because species can be traced to fossils from the Cretaceous, Eocene and Jurassic period. The largest bowfin caught in Michigan, and the state record, weighed 14 pounds.

Northern snakeheads have a parabronchial organ (a primitive lung) that allows them to breathe air, enabling them to survive in low-oxygen waters and even on land for up to four days if kept moist. They can move on land by wriggling their bodies and using their pectoral fins, allowing them to migrate between water bodies. They are fairly cold-tolerant and can survive winters in many parts of the United States, including under ice.

White Bass range in color from a silvery white to a pale green. Their backs are mostly black, while their sides and belly are pale with stripes running along them. White Bass are related to Striped Bass and called wipers. The largest white bass caught in Michigan weighed 6.44 pounds, Length: 21.9 inches.

Lake whitefish are related to salmon and trout. They are known for their deep-bodied, silvery appearance and are a major part of the Great Lakes ecosystem. They typically grow to 17-22 inches and range from 1.5-4 pounds. Whitefish are a popular and valuable commercial fish, generating the greatest income for Great Lakes commercial fisheries. Lake whitefish are also known as Lake Superior whitefish, whiting, and shad. The largest lake whitefish caught in Michigan weighed 14 pounds, 4.48 ounces.

Lake Sturgeons have sharp spines on their back, so be careful when handling them. Instead of scales, sturgeon skin is covered in bony plates called scutes, which can be very sharp on young sturgeon. Sturgeons have been around since the dinosaur days. Sturgeons mostly live in large, freshwater lakes and rivers. Their average lifespan is 50 to 60 years. The biggest sturgeon recorded in Michigan weighed 193 pounds and measured 88 inches long.

There are few different species of Gar, the Longnose gar, Short nose and Alligator gar. The Long Nose Gar got its name because of its long mouth that looks like an alligator's mouth. The alligator gar is one of the biggest freshwater fish growing up to 10 feet long. The world record for a catch was set at 327 pounds. The largest longnose gar caught in Michigan weighed 18 pounds.

The burbot, also known as the eel pout. They get their name because they have a serpent-like or eel-like body. They can wrap their tail around things. There's nothing to worry about if you catch one, they may try to wrap their tail around your arm, but they are harmless. Burbots are adapted to cold water and are found in large, cold rivers, lakes, and reservoirs, primarily preferring freshwater habitats. Burbots are also known as eelpout, lingcod, and lawyer. The largest burbot caught in Michigan weighed 18.25 pounds.

Male freshwater drum make a rumbling or grunting sound by contracting muscles along their air bladder walls. They have large, ivory-like ear bones that can be up to an inch in diameter, which Native Americans used as necklaces or bracelets and sometimes referred to as the lucky stones. Freshwater drum are primarily bottom feeders, spending much of their time near the bottom of lakes and rivers in search of food. The largest freshwater drum caught in Michigan weighed 28.61 pounds, Length: 34.02 inches.

Carp have long been an important food fish to humans. Carp are bottom feeders for the most part and their mouth is made like a suction cup, so they can suck food off the bottom. Carp are good for a lake because they help clean the bottom of the lake. The largest carp caught in Michigan, weighed an estimated 65 pounds.

Brook trout are characterized by their olive-green bodies with pale, worm-like markings, red spots with bluish halos, and orange-red fins with white and black edges. They can grow up to 12 inches in length. Brook trout are cold-water fish that prefer clean, clear, and cold streams, lakes, and ponds. The largest recorded brook trout caught in Michigan weighed 9.5 pounds and was 28.1 inches long.

The lake trout is one of the biggest of the trout family. The biggest lake trout caught was 72 pounds. Lake trout like to live in lakes that are deep. They like being in the cool water in the deep parts of a lake. They have been reported to live up to 70 years in some Canadian lakes. The largest lake trout caught in Michigan weighed 61.5 pounds.

Brown trout can live up to 20 years. Brown trout have higher tolerance for warmer waters than either brook or rainbow trout. Brown trout can be found on almost every continent except Antarctica, and many can be found living in the ocean. The largest brown trout caught in Michigan weighed 41 pounds, 7.25 ounces, Length 43.75 inches.

Chinook also known as the king salmon are the most widespread Salmon in North America. Chinook salmon are hatch in freshwater streams and rivers then migrate out to the saltwater environment of the ocean to feed and grow. Chinook salmon are the largest of the Pacific Ocean salmon, that's how they got the name king salmon. The largest Chinook salmon ever caught in Michigan, weighing 47.86 pounds and measuring 47.5 inches.

Coho salmon, also known as silver salmon, are fish that live in both freshwater and saltwater, migrating from the ocean to their natal streams to spawn, where they die shortly after. Some coho salmon migrate more than 1,000 miles in the ocean, while others remain in marine areas close to the streams where they were born. Adult coho salmon typically weigh 8 to 12 pounds and are 24 to 30 inches long, but some can reach up to 36 pounds. The largest Coho salmon caught in Michigan weighed 47.86 pounds.

The Arctic grayling is one of the most beautiful freshwater fishes. Its most striking physical feature is the large, sail like dorsal or backfin. The Arctic grayling comes in a wide array of colors. Their color can vary from stream to stream. The sides of the body, fins and head can be freckled with spots. They can grow to be 30 inches long and weigh up to 8.4 pounds. They can travel more than 100 miles in one year. The largest Arctic grayling caught in Michigan weighed 8.4 pounds and measured 30 inches in length.

Smallmouth bass have a smaller mouth than the largemouth bass. They also have different markings and are lighter in color. They don't live in most lakes because they prefer living in colder water. They are typically found in the northern states in America because the water is cooler. The current world record smallmouth is an 11-pound, 15-ounce fish caught in Dale Hollow Lake. The largest smallmouth bass caught in Michigan, and the current state record, weighed 9.98 pounds.

The largemouth bass is the most sought-after bass in North America. Largemouth bass live in just about every lake in North America. They have great hearing and can hear a crayfish crawling on the bottom of the lake. The biggest largemouth bass caught in Michigan weighed 11 pounds, 15 ounces, Length 27 inches.

The sauger is part of the walleye family. There are 2 different types of saugers. The normal sauger and the suageye. The saugeye is a mix of the sauger and walleye. The suageye have white eyes just like the walleye. The sauger and suageye are smaller than the walleye. Saugers are more likely to be found in large rivers with deep pools but are also found in lakes.

The walleye got its name because of its white looking eyes. Their eyes collect light, even in low light conditions. This means they can see in the dark. Because they can see in the dark, they mostly feed at night. During the daytime their eyes are very sensitive, so they usually head for deeper water or shady places. Walleye like to live in cooler water and are normally found in the upper part of North America. The largest walleye caught in Michigan, on record, weighed 17.19 pounds and measured 35 inches long.

Pickerel kind of look like northern pike, but they are not. The Pike is larger in size than the Pickerel. The Pickerel has more spots than the Pike, but the Pike has spots on its fins and pickerel don't. Pickerel has a dark bar beneath their eyes and northern pike don't. Pickerel are also known as gunfish or slime darts. The largest chain pickerel caught in Michigan weighed 9 pounds, 6 ounces.

The Northern Pike is one of the most sought-after fish for anglers. It got its name because it likes to live in cooler water mainly in the northern states of North America. The northern pike is a very aggressive predator. They don't like to live in groups with other fish, they are very territorial and like to live alone. Their behavior is closely affected by weather conditions. The Michigan state record for a Northern Pike is a 39-pounds and 51.5-inches long.

The muskellunge called the Musky or Muskie for short is one of the biggest game fish in freshwater lakes. The largest on record was 69 pounds, 15 ounces. The Muskie likes to live in cooler water and can be found in most lakes in the upper part of north America. Anglers look at Muskellunges as trophy fish. They are hard to catch, there's a saying that it takes a thousand casts to catch one. The largest muskellunge caught in Michigan was a 58-pounds and 58-inches long.

Another breed of the Muskie is the tiger muskie. The tiger muskie is a cross between the northern pike and muskie. They grow larger and faster than normal muskies and northern pikes. The tiger muskie got its name because it has tiger like stripes. Tiger Muskies are very rare and hard to catch. The largest tiger muskie caught in Michigan, on record, weighed 51 pounds.

Fun Facts About Michigan Fish

1 - In 1988, the Michigan Legislature specified the Brook Trout as the state fish.

2 - Unlike other salmon, the brook trout lack teeth on the roof of their mouth.

3 - The lake sturgeon are the granddaddy of Michigan fish. They can live up to 100 years and weigh up to 200 pounds.

4 - Walleye are a favorite target for anglers, and the largest member of the perch family.

5 - Salmon are popular in Michigan's angling scene, particularly in the Great Lakes and their tributaries.

6 - The burbot, also known as eelpout, is a member of the freshwater cod family and has an odd habit of wrapping its slimy tail around the hand or arm of anglers.

7 – White sucker is the most common and abundant fish in Michigan.

Author Page

Billy Grinslott & Kinsey Marie Books

ISBN – 9781965098806

Thanks

www.ingramcontent.com/pod-product-compliance
Lightning Source LLC
Chambersburg PA
CBHW060851270326
41934CB00002B/89